ALLUSIONS

by
M.H. VESSEUR

ALLUSIONS

A collection of short stories by
M.H. VESSEUR

Vibes Publishing

Second edition
ISBN 978-94-91908-27-9 (paperback, 2nd edition)
ISBN 978-94-91908-10-1 (Kindle epub with DRM)
ISBN 978-94-91908-11-8 (epub)

Published by Vibes
www.mhvesseur.com

ALLUSIONS

Contents

Preface

We never saw reality coming. It reveals itself to us at the last possible moment, every morning, always unexpected, always indelible, never foreseen. We should have looked better, some say.

I hardly ever share that sentiment. The extrapolation of the present reveals much of what awaits us, and if we follow that direction we find ourselves in an imaginary landscape that resembles a more believable future than that of statistics and common sense. Many of my short stories have been the result of that process.

There is a slight problem with this approach. It's the willingness of the reader to look at the enlarged themes and go along with the author, something I can not take for granted. In their introduction to the unique work by J.G. Ballard, The Atrocity Exhibition, Andrea Juno and V. Vale refer to a statement made by William S. Burroughs, which has always inspired me and is an appropriate point to make here: "The best way to keep something bad from happening is to see it ahead of time... and you can't see it if you refuse to face the possibility."

This path led me, for the first time, to the creation of a short story that sort of blew up our current economic system to the size of, what I called, the Super Economy. The result was not appreciated by all readers. The editors of the magazine that published that first story were divided: half of them loved the piece, the other half loathed it. I consider that a recurring compliment in my career, and it also proves my point. (That particular story, The Burning of Neil Armstrong, is included in this revised second edition of Allusions.)

So I stayed on course and wrote a series of extrapolating stories about themes I felt were relevant to our times as well as the near future. Many of these stories were received with similar ambivalence, but I've always clung to the half of my audience that was willing to make any strange journey with me. So what kind of world emerges from this way of traveling into the near future?

The question What will our entertainment industry lead us to in the long run? resulted in the first piece of this collection: In Snuff Park. There is surely nothing beyond this point; the evolution of entertainment has been completed, and we can rightfully claim, referring to Neil Postman, that we are "amusing ourselves to death."

Next in Allusions is the theme of eternal beauty, and youth. We will soon be able to extend life far beyond our current horizon, be it by cloning or by sustaining the bodies we're born into. But I am convinced it is not eternity we're after. It's beauty and youth. The longer we live, the bigger the effort, and I've written Babyface Junkie in that spirit. There is a price to pay for anything that lasts. Inspiration came, as you will find out, from artists dealing with beauty all over the arts:

Thomas Mann, Stanley Kubrick, Steven Spielberg, Christiane F. You name it.

The next story, Narcissist Guru, deals with the ego and the way we as individuals can drown in the media sea. But there's more going on; this story has a tendency to incorporate other themes as well.

Further down the line, art comes into view as something more than to just stare at numbly in a museum. For a long time I was — and still am — mesmerized by the artistry of Christo and Jeanne-Claude, by the way they could change an object in public space and turn it into something else. Whenever a new installation was opened for the public, it changed the atmosphere, it changed the location for a short period in time, and it did so more powerful — for a variety of reasons — than a normal exhibition inside a museum. It was this changing of the public space that took possession of me and wouldn't let go. The result was Sketches of a Worldwide Christo and Jeanne-Claude, a story that, I'm proud to say, received the artists' acclaim.

The next story, Territory Game, engages the future in a more literal form. Sooner or later technology is going to render most of nature redundant. In Blade Runner, the landmark film by Ridley Scott, based on the novel Do Androids Dream of Electric Sheep by Philip K. Dick, an artificial owl is considered nothing special, a cloned fake, just one step away from an entirely synthetic life form. What's to keep us from creating nylon oxygen, to quote the Intergalactic Radio Station as created by Vangelis on his album Direct? And again, what starts out to be beautiful, soon rears its ugly head.

The final story moves to a more personal level, which ties this preface back to its beginning, the part where we never saw the future coming. And that is precisely what the heroin of Beloved Stalker must feel.

This concise selection of my short stories is not necessarily a pretty sight, but it puts me at ease. We can take comfort in the notion that fiction can never be more barbaric than reality. That much we've learned after more than twenty centuries since we started counting. It seems only natural that any form of speculation about where we're going ends in flames. If your pages start to burn while you read them, or if your device becomes too hot to handle, I am convinced you are on the right track.

Meanwhile I continue to follow my own tracks and hope to find myself in a world were everything is extrapolated. That way we can see the world around us anew, and wake up from our catatonic submission to the reality of modern times.

M.H. Vesseur

ALLUSIONS

In Snuff Park

I

The operator lights up his usual forbidden cigarette and for a moment watches the opening sequences in cinema 84, in the darkness on the other side of the soundproof glass.

II

The jury report of the Cannes Documentary Film Festival concludes: "The documentary 'In Snuff Park' takes too long to get moving to seize our attention. What good are exquisite opening shots if the audience is groping in the dark? Today's zappers are bored by art cinema."

III

Far from Cannes, in Snuff Park, a visitor takes a deep breath at the main gate. There is a smell of death, but he doesn't know what death smells like.

IV

In cinema 84 a desert appears out of inky black nothingness, only vaguely visible in the blood-red light of a dusky sun.

Shafts of laser beams and flashes from fireworks soar upwards and illuminate a walled city of domes, castles and rollers coasters, half protruding above the fence. By the gate, at the edge of vast parking lots, on tall poles, scores of flags keep the logo of the theme park carefully hidden in their satin folds.

V

The commentator's voice reminds him vaguely of one of those Shakespearean giants whom young people no longer remember: John Gielgud. While he tries to picture the actor's face, the operator sits with his back to the glass, cap down over his eyes, nodding off in the projectionist's chair. He can tell perfectly well by the sound piped from the auditorium if everything is O.K.

The benevolent, bronze vibrato of the Gielgud voice soothes him: "In the desert life and death are inexorable. So those who conceived Snuff Park could have found no better setting for their ideas than the desolation of this desert. Some eight million customers have already made the trip to this region, to visit the only amusement park in the world that has never needed to advertise. Through this gate young and old from all over the world enter fraternally for the experience of a lifetime. Those waiting in line wave their admission tickets, designed in the style of summonses from the federal court. Just a short wait and the gate of what has been called the world's most exciting amusement park will swing open for everyone aged eighteen and over."

VI

"Jolene and Wilbur Macy from North Dakota are on their

honeymoon. The attraction that has caught their eye is called the Injection. It is now twelve noon and Jolene and Wilbur will have to queue for another hour and a half. The Macy's don't seem to mind; they have been in the queue since eight-thirty. Waiting is standard in Snuff Park, according to the PR spokesperson purely to pile on the suspense. Although they have been warned in the brochure and on the admission ticket, many people are very disappointed when they reach the computer operated board giving waiting times. 127 minutes for the 'Head-On Collision' ride, 300 minutes for the 'Air Crash' roller coaster, 500 minutes for the 'Date Rape" attraction, 45 minutes for 'Serial Killer', 241 minutes for the 'Injection', 200 minutes for the 'Gas Chamber', 645 minutes for the 'Electric Chair', 23 minutes for 'Firing Squad', and so on. Patience is a deadly business, as they say here."

VII

"The Grindmans – Bernie and Alexiana from Pennsylvania – are standing outside the courthouse, discussing how they can best spend their visit to Snuff Park. These are the connoisseurs, the visitors with a season ticket. Ordinary customers head straight for the usual attractions, but Bernie and Alexiana want the works. They choose an armed robbery with a killing, a trial lasting a whole day and finally the Electric Chair. The first part of their programme will be played out this afternoon with a number of actors. Using rubber bullets and large quantities of stage blood they will convince the Grindmans of their own murderousness, in the course of perfectly re-enacted scenes from 'Natural Born Killers'. Tomorrow they will appear in court for a trial indistinguishable from the real thing, where they will face the death penalty. The assistance of celebrated lawyers is included in the price and the pleas are based on actual legal practice. The third and final day – Bernie and Alexiana will spend the night in Death Row Hotel – is reserved for the demanding programme of the harrowing major attraction that they have been looking forward to for months: the Electric Chair. At eleven a.m. they will be escorted into the execution room. Half an hour later, they will have been dressed in the clean white overalls of the amusement park and will have taken a sedative. At one p.m. the chair will be prepared. Then, until two o'clock, there will be a flurry of calls to family and official bodies to make the illusion of guilt and sentencing as real as possible. Then the chaplain will appear for a last visit, followed by twelve witnesses. At three p.m. the director of the attraction reads out the sentence and the execution begins. Everything is timed with a stopwatch and recorded in writing and on film for their personal memento DVD."

VIII

"For their 'last words' visitors can seek help from the Famous Last Words Pavilion in Snuff Park. Here millions of utterances made by celebrities and nameless individuals, whether or not on their deathbed, are held on computer. One can also draw on millions of quotations from literature, pop music, poetry, science, religion and politics. Bernie has made his choice and is practising in the audio room."

For a moment the the commentary gives way to a deep, smoky voice with a Mid-West accent: "It's a small step for mankind, but a giant leap for a man!"

The operator opens his eyes again. He recognises this line. Where on earth was it from? 'Walking on the Moon' by the Police?

He drifts off again. It'll come back to him.

IX

"This is Bernie's *Night on Death Row*. The men he is talking to here are not visitors to the theme park. Nor are they management or staff. These men really have been sentenced to death by the courts of their home states and are awaiting execution here. John, found guilty of murder in the course of a robbery, Gerald, a three-time sex murderer, Romma, a serial killer. Plus seven others. The have agreed to spend their remaining years of trials and appeals and waiting in Snuff Park and to give visitors a sense of what death row really means. John, Gerald en Romma are obviously getting on well with their guest, happy to be admired for once for their violent past. They take their time over their stories."

X

"From the juke box in the execution room, as background music for his short stay in the electric chair and for his memento DVD Bernie chooses 'My Way' by Frank Sinatra, 'Electric Avenue' by Eddy Grant, the opening theme from the soundtrack of 'Close Encounters of the Third Kind' by John Williams. 'Una Paloma Blanca' from the George Baker Selection – the song once requested by the world's most famous condemned man Gary Gilmore – can be listened to completely free of copyright by visitors to Snuff Park."

XI

At the first notes of 'Una Paloma Blanca' the operator opens his eyes. He thinks of his father, seated at the kitchen table on the coast of the South of France, decades ago, and of the sounds of the bandoneon. Sucking and blowing noises and the virtuosity of an amateur. Then he pushes his cap still deeper over his forehead and closes his eyes again. Anyway, behind his back it is business as usual.

Still about three-quarters of an hour to go to the change of film.

XII

Doove. Doove.

"These two dull thumps mark the beginning of the execution. The current has been switched on. Bernie has been looking forward to this for ages. He has saved up for six months for this and gone without a holiday. Consequently he starts when he hears these sounds. As far as he *can* start, that is, since all those straps and buckles hold him firmly in place in the electric chair. So what you see is not so much Bernie's enthusiasm at hearing this starting gun as it were. It is purely a muscular reaction to the power surge. Due to the variable current, from a very high voltage to a low one and back again, Bernie's muscles contract powerfully. Spine straight, head thrown back, fingers stretched – everything that can move is galvanised by a massive cramp. Bernie is completely unconscious by now. At least that is the intention. By the time the pain signals from the nerves reach his brain, the brain is already out of action. He gradually subsides until a new maximum voltage is applied. Behind the glass Alexiana looks on and remembers the words her husband uttered earlier that day: 'What do you get when you add volts and amperes? Voltaire!'"

Doove.

"And Bernie is sitting up again. Ten thousand volts are racing through his body. The steam you can see comes from the wet sponges attached to the electrodes under the leather cap on his head. It's really beginning to heat up under there!"

The operator frowns. His eyes remain closed. He cannot get back to sleep. In the silence that the voiceover of the documentary allows to fall, he can finally hear the background music properly. In all the long years he has spent in this job his main pastime has been identifying the music in the features and documentaries he projects. Or the composer. That's why he is the best: he stays at his post during the projection. That's a bit different from the new generation, who after getting things started go off for a coffee and don't return before the interval. Gradually he has learned that Vangelis, Pink Floyd and Brian Eno are big favourites with documentary makers. He had often heard 'To the Unknown Man', 'Shine on you Crazy Diamond' and 'Music for Airports' on the soundtrack. But what is this music? It's a bit like John Williams. 'Minority Report'? What title did that guy, that Bernie mention?

"The sparks and flames you can see jumping twenty centimetres above Bernie's head, are not part of the execution protocol. We asked the supervisor of the Electric Chair attraction what happened."

"What you see here," says an enthusiastic, well-trained voice, "is a slight overloading of the circuits as a result of excess liquid content in the body of visitor Bernie Grindman, probably caused by too high a coffee intake before the execution. The blood that you can see running down his cheek, comes from the left eye, which has been forced out of its socket by the excessive build-up of steam. As long as his brain does not reach boiling point, there is no cause for concern."

In an ensuing silence, swelling, melodious tones can be heard. The operator starts. "Got it," he mutters, "'Close Encounters' by Williams. Great."

A majestic boom, produced by having the scores of instruments in the orchestra sound simultaneously, vibrates through the speakers and through the glass of the projection room.

"It's over. The doctor officially certifies Bernie as dead."

XIII

The operator looks round for a moment on hearing Bernie's voice, surprised by the uncertain enunciation and weary sound.

"You know, the reanimation went very well, just as I expected, you know, they always do an excellent job here, these doctors at Snuff Park are the best neurologists, cardiologists and plastic surgeons around, they patch up hundreds of visitors every day, very smart, very professional. That's the thing, you know. Right, my left eye has to be replaced, as it ruptured, but if that's all, I'm satisfied, you know things like that can happen. Still got a bit of a headache, as bad as that time the Knacks lost to the Sox, you know. Anyway I'm in a lot better shape than the first time I went to the chair, this time I worked out a lot in the gym so I pulled as few muscles as possible. Terrific."

XIV

"By evening of this second day the queue for the Electric Chair has become considerably shorter. Some people want to sit in the chair and be executed without the trial and all the extras Bernie opted for. Others, though, want to be the executioner and carry out the sentence. Still others want to be spectators or witnesses."

XV

The digital watch glows faintly in the dim light. That must be more or less it, thinks the operator, getting up.

"And so another day ends in Snuff Park. And what a day. Seven hundred dead, six hundred and eighty-nine successful reanimations. Satisfied visitors swarm across the parking lots and hotels of the complex. All with their own Snuff Movie DVD in their pocket. Their souvenir to take home. Because how else are the folks back home to believe that your vacation was to die for?"

***

Babyface Junkie

I. THE BIRTHDAYS IN MY LIFE.

In 2003, I celebrated my first birthday. In 2004, I celebrated my second birthday. In 2005, I celebrated my third birthday. In 2006, I celebrated my fourth birthday. In 2007, I celebrated my fifth birthday. In 2008, I celebrated my sixth birthday. In 2009, I celebrated my seventh birthday. In 2010, I celebrated my eighth birthday. In 2011, I celebrated my ninth birthday. In 2012, I celebrated my tenth birthday. In 2013, I celebrated my eleventh birthday. In 2014, I celebrated my twelfth birthday. In 2015, I celebrated my thirteenth birthday. In 2016, I celebrated my fourteenth birthday. In 2017, I celebrated my fifteenth birthday. In 2018, I celebrated my sixteenth birthday. In 2019, I celebrated my seventeenth birthday. In 2020, I celebrated my seventeenth birthday. In 2021, I celebrated my seventeenth birthday. In 2022, I celebrated my seventeenth birthday. In 2023, I celebrated my seventeenth birthday. In 2024, I celebrated my seventeenth birthday. In 2025, I celebrated my seventeenth birthday. In 2026, I celebrated my seventeenth birthday. In 2027, I celebrated my seventeenth birthday. In 2028, I celebrated my seventeenth birthday. In 2029, I celebrated my seventeenth birthday. In 2030, I celebrated my seventeenth birthday. In 2031, I celebrated my seventeenth birthday. In 2032, I celebrated my seventeenth birthday. In 2033, I celebrated my seventeenth birthday. In 2034, I celebrated my seventeenth birthday. In 2035, I celebrated my seventeenth birthday. In 2036, I celebrated my seventeenth birthday. In 2037, I celebrated my seventeenth birthday my first birthday. In 2038, I celebrated my seventeenth birthday. In 2039, I celebrated my seventeenth birthday. In 2040, I celebrated my seventeenth birthday. In 2041, I celebrated my seventeenth birthday. In 2042, I celebrated my seventeenth birthday. And in 2043, I shall celebrate my seventeenth birthday. (From the letters column of *Time* magazine.)

II. PHOTO CAPTIONS.
Photo 1. Julia and her boyfriend Gunnar in the year when they reached the legal age of seventeen.

Photo 2. Julia and Gunnar outside the Ever Young Clinic in Gstaad.

Photo 3. Dr Georg at Julia's bedside, the day before the treatment.

Photo 4. Julia in the garden of the clinic, a few days after the treatment.

Photo 5. Julia with the First Lady of the USA, at the time the world's most famous AY (Artificial Youth) recipient. From left to right: President Tom Cruise (71), Julia (legal age 22, artificial age 17) and First Lady Marisa Callissario (legal age 69, artificial age 21).

Photo 6. Julia on vacation in Monacoco-Chanel, in the bathroom with the hypodermic syringe containing her daily dose of Youth Restoring Enzyme CF.

Photo 7. With fellow-fashion models at Club YSL in Monacoco-Chanel.

Photo 8. Julia at home with Gunnar. Gunnar is now fifty-two, Julia is still seventeen, with a legal age of fifty-two.

Photo 9. Julia at the legal age of fifty-five with new boyfriend Riud (19), after her divorce from Gunnar.

Photo 10. Publicity shot for Julia's first porn movie, also starring Riud.

Photo 11. Julia, six months after her bankruptcy, in the red-light district of Paris. An interested customer can be seen through the window of his Mercedes-Benz. Julia's legal age at this point is sixty.

III. CASE NUMBER 20-209100-21.
Amsterdam Criminal Court. Judgement in the criminal proceedings against Julia Guardiano, born in Amsterdam, resident in Paris.

    The indictment. The Court is persuaded and deems it to

have been proven beyond reasonable doubt that in coastal areas of European Union member states between approximately 20 January and 20 October the accused maintained an intimate relationship (as defined in the case of G. Vandenhove vs. the European Union) with the minor Paolo de P. The sexual acts falling under existing child abuse legislation were committed on the dates listed in Supplement 4, on a total of 97 confirmed occasions. In view of the legal age of the accused at this time (82) the intimate part of the aforesaid relationship must be classed as child abuse. It is argued by the defence that while the accused has a legal age of eighty-two, she has the appearance of a seventeen-year-old – being an *artificial youth* recipient as defined in the Nuremberg Age Laws. Hence Paolo de P. saw her as the same age as himself, with an advantage that was invisible to him. The indictment is therefore misrepresentation and abuse.

Judgement. The Court:

Finds that the artificial age of the accused is not relevant in this case, since it relates only to external appearance. The Child Abuse Act states that adults are in a superior position to minors by virtue of their experience and social position and in that capacity can easily sexually abuse minors. The artificial age has no bearing on experience and social position and in that sense the accused, notwithstanding, has the age of eighty-two.

Finds the proven indictment punishable in law, qualifies this as previously stated, and finds the accused guilty.

Sentences the accused to prison for a period of 13 (thirteen) years.

Orders that the time spent by the accused in custody and

on remand prior to the passing of sentence be deducted from the period of confinement.

By order of the Court: His Honour Mr Nanninckhoof, chairman, Their Honours Cuijck and Zomers, judges, in the presence of Mr Van Hoorn, clerk of the court, this 24th day of January 85, meeting in open session.

IV. ADVERTISING COPY.

Small top header: Real doctors, real science, real results!

Large header: Does your age really make a difference to your lover?

Smaller headers below: More than you can ever imagine. But the Stay Young Method makes an even bigger difference! *Eternal Youth Breakthrough*.

Main body of text: YOUTH RESTORING ENZYME CF® is definitely the simplest and fastest medically endorsed way of preventing physical ageing. And of ensuring your lover stays in love ever after. In love ... with you! Just one week in the Ever Young Clinic in Gstaad and you will stay as you are – all your life. To the very end defeat the merciless biological clock that ages you. Watched by your admiring partner face the onslaught of new generations with astonishing ease. No cell therapy, no facelift, no super vitamin cure is more effective than Youth Restoring Enzyme CF®. Proven in the lives of many couples: keeps love alive!

Text in box: The doctor behind YOUTH RESTORING ENZYME CF® is Dr Georg Aguil, MD, a qualified gerontologist who has already freed 70,000 patients from physical ageing. He is a member of both the College of Gerontology and the Society of Gerontology and heads a team of forty-six gerontologists. After seven years of tests Dr Aguil made the astonishing discovery now known as YOUTH RESTORING ENZYME CF®, a 100 per cent natural youth restoring formula. Unlike the old, completely synthetic Polyester Enzyme PE method, YOUTH RESTORING ENZYME CF® can actually be used until natural death from old age occurs. Dr Aguil's team of dedicated biologists and biochemists work with the naturally occurring mould FUNGUSCIANE-F, which helps restore sections of DNA broken down as a result of old age. FUNGUSCIANE-F mould also supplements the growth hormone Somatomedine in the body, sufficiently to reduce the ageing effect of the latter, without this leading to dwarfism in young people. As a result the treatment can be used as early as adolescence.

Text in box: Nothing else ever needed! In one week a basic dose of YOUTH RESTORING ENZYME CF® is administered. This is carried out by clinicians in the Ever Young Clinic in Gstaad, in special thermal baths through daily intravenous injections. Thereafter one dose a day, intravenous, is sufficient. May be administered painlessly by the patient with the automatic, portable Enzymator ®, in a travel case.

Text in box: Comments from some satisfied youthful customers:

"I've felt so beautiful for the last twenty years! Thanks to YOUTH RESTORING ENZYME CF®."

"My husband is in his late sixties now and enjoys the admiring looks: everyone is jealous of the older man with his stunning young girlfriend. And all without divorce or alimony!"

Text at bottom: Book your treatment now. Call freephone

9-000-722-008-#0#. Or e-mail your credit card number to reservations@ever-young. And visit our website at www.ever-young.com.

V. WARNINGS FROM ANOTHER AGE.
"Because of the sweet youth inflicted on him, he was disgusted by his aging body."
— Thomas Mann, *Death in Venice*, 1911

"The needle was still sticking in my arm. I had a blinding headache. At first I couldn't stand up. I thought that was it, I was going to die."
— Christiane F., *We Children of Zoo Station*, 1978

"Do not be fooled by the artistry of this creation."
— Steven Spielberg, *A.I.*, 2001

VI. MIRROR OF YOUTH.
Never before in the fifty years that the research programme had been in progress had such a blazing row erupted. The team of gerontologists only just managed to prevent the monozygotic twins Rosalynd and Ariane from attacking each other. What had triggered the discord was the point touched on in passing by the team leader, Dr Georg Aguil, MD. It concerned a worldwide publicity campaign for the university where he conducted his research. A star photographer was to capture the sisters in a harmonious pose. This photograph would be syndicated to every major magazine and newspaper as the first objective proof of the properties of the enzyme. A

world tour was also on the cards, all part of the promotion of the university.

But Rosalynd's patience with the research was running out. The adventurous teenager from the beginning of the project was now an elderly woman of sixty-seven. Rosalynd's resemblance to her still youthful twin sister faded with each passing year. For years the suspicion had been growing in her that she had made a dreadful mistake.

In response to Dr Georg's proposal Rosalynd told him in no uncertain terms that she didn't mind growing old. But she did not want to be held up to the whole world as a shameful example of the havoc played by age if one rejected Dr Georg's enzyme. If the world attached more importance to Ariane's phoney youth than to her genuine old age and wisdom, said Rosalynd, there was obviously no longer any place for her on this earth.

Shaking his head, Dr Georg went to his office, leaving the neurotically quarrelling siblings to the care of his team. If Rosalynd rejected even an ordinary advertising campaign, what on earth would her attitude be to his plan to preserve the twins in formaldehyde after their death and to build a museum around them?

It was time to let the lawyers loose on the case again.

VII. THE AAA NEWSLETTER.
Quotes from the newsletter of Artificial Adolescents Anonymous:

"I had the treatment because the publisher of Vogue paid for me. The clinic in Gstaad, the daily injections. For twenty years, till

M.H. Vesseur

they were sick of my babyface. I work as a call girl now, to earn the money for the injections. I've looked like a fifteen-year-old for twenty years now, but it's no big deal any more." — Gisele B. (15, legal age 35)

"A couturier at YSL fell in love with me and got the fashion house to finance the treatment. I've been seventeen for twenty years, but I can't get modelling work any more. I've stayed the same, but of course the ideal look hasn't. I can only afford the injections because my parents left me plenty of money." — Didier S. (17, legal age 37)

"I've had a babyface for thirty-seven years, but it hasn't given me the security I was hoping for. My husband left me for a woman his own age. What's more, someone who actually looks her age, he said. As for me, I've no friends left, because I give people the creeps: I look younger than my daughter!" — Carol C. (21, legal age 58)

"I've had a computer simulation done so I can see myself old. I wanted to know what I might have looked like now I'm nearly eighty. I've lived for sixty years in the body of the teenager I once was, but I've had enough." — Carine R. (18, legal age 78)

"People of my own generation reject me, because my eternal youth reminds them of their lost adolescence. But younger people don't want me either. Close relationships never last long. Whenever a girlfriend finds out I inject myself, she ends it." — Christopher C. (21, legal age 68)

"*Detlev and I have lived downtown for years, picking up customers in the underground to pay for our daily ampoule of CF near the Rijksmuseum. We shoot up behind the Van Gogh Museum, or if there's any money left in a hotel. We've got to stay young. We've stayed so beautiful!*" — Esmee L. (20, legal age 30)

"*Since I stopped the daily CF injections six months ago, it's been a living hell. The growth hormones have it all their own way again and it's as if they're taking revenge. I'm growing too fast in some places, too slowly in others, so that dwarfism is occurring. I can't describe the pain. A doctor in emergency says I haven't long to live.*" — Nancy P. (23, legal age 29)

"*Dear AAA friends, not even you can help me any longer. It's my own fault. I was paid by Revlon to have all that enzyme crap injected into my body. For ten years my life was a dream. I was on every cover, till Revlon terminated my contract. By the time you read this, I shall have ended my life in the place where they robbed me of it: outside the main entrance of the Revlon Corporation on Madison Avenue.*" — Tirza J. (30, legal age at death 45)

VIII. TELEPHONE ORDER.
Type: Central European marble.

Size: H 2.00 m x W 0.95 m x D 0.10 m.

Lettering: Times New Roman.

Text in capitals: "Only beauty is at once divine and visible."
— Thomas Mann.

Text in lower case: "Isabelle Gaveau, 2013 – 2088. Here lies my beloved Isabelle, forever seventeen. François."

***

Narcissist Guru

The performance. I am one of the few people still alive to have seen the Narcissist Guru™ as he really was. The front of the invitation, now twenty-seven years old, yellowed, wrinkled and covered in coffee stains, still proclaims in glossy type: *Through the Mirror We Search for Ourselves*. Inside the reader is invited to visit the artist's house. The house, at the time not yet a museum, was covered almost completely in reflective glass or reflective paint and mirrored its surrounds from every conceivable angle. The walls assumed the shapes of the trees, the bushes, the grass and the swimming pool in the garden. The roof was one with the blue sky and the clouds. The front door presented the visitor first and foremost with an image of himself.

Behind the house a stand of steel tubes was constructed on a concrete platform. Beyond the platform stretched the garden, full of small trees clipped into globe shapes, bushes like obelisks, pools and gravel paths. Laid out in a strict symmetrical pattern: from the concrete platform a path led at right-angles into the garden as far as the ivy-covered garden wall about two hundred metres away. The two sides of the path were each other's mirror image. Every path, every pool, every tree gazed silently at its alter ego on the other side.

The garden served only as a backdrop, since the performance took place entirely on the concrete platform. Sitting in the stand we looked down on an oblong wooden container in front of us. A kind of bathtub, but without the usual rounded edges that offer comfort to the human body. The width of the structure actually approximated a bathtub in size. The length, though, was very different and was at least five metres. *Also sprach Zarathustra* blared from the PA system as the artist appeared from the house. He mounted a small flight of steps and stopped at the end of the wooden container. Then he looked straight ahead, at his audience. Ahead of him stretched five metres of motionless water. The surface reflected with great intensity, as if the container had been filled with mercury. He looked down at his reflected self at his feet.

Then he moved a foot forward till it was a fraction above the foot moved forward by his mirror image, and lowered it slowly into the water. In doing so he also created a new definition of the word slow. Not a ripple broke free and disturbed the surface of the water. As his foot dissolved into the foot of his reflection, the guru began to speak.

'We have been searching for so long for who we are.'

His leg stopped once his foot had completely disappeared, resting on an invisible step below the unfathomable surface. His leg merged seamlessly with that of his mirrored self, which stared at us upside down. Now his other leg followed.

'We have found nothing.'

The other two feet merged in the motionless surface.

'Nor will we ever find what we are looking for. Because where we were looking, there is nothing but a world lying fallow.'

The artist descended the invisible steps extremely slowly. His legs became shorter and shorter. He seemed to be melting from below like an iceman.

'We must cease the search outside ourselves and turn inwards.'

I can still remember his hands and how they hung motionless at his side. His fingertips touched the dish of mercury in which his lower body had already dissolved. His mirror image let his hands hang upwards – from our perspective – so that the fingers touched, merged, and became one.

'We were created from the inside of god, from an inward god, and only inside can we find answers to our questions about creation.'

Slowly, for almost an hour, the artist descended. Occasionally speaking, at other times allowing the music to speak for itself, as it was turned up and then down by an invisible hand, without any prearranged signal. Finally the two chins merged and the man spoke his final words.

'In order to be able to free ourselves from ourselves we must first descend into ourselves.'

For the last ten minutes he was silent, the music stopped and a silent public looked at the two merging heads with the closed eyes on the surface of the container.

Then there began an endless intermezzo, preceding a presumed ending. The bushes and the clouds were reflected in the place where the Narcissist Guru™ had disappeared.

After a few minutes panic broke out. A few members of the audience darted forward. They rushed to the container and groped around wildly in the liquid that spattered in shiny droplets, and dragged the artist out of the water.

A completely new performance was created: the resuscitation of a drowned man.

The bill portrait. A few times during my days at the Museum I met the reclusive billionaire A.O. He always stood in the same room and stared at the bill portrait. More precisely, he stared at himself in the bill portrait.

Once, when he was not there, I went and had a look for myself. In the middle of the room was a panel. It was about one and a half metres wide and reached up to the ceiling. On the floor behind the panel two footprints were painted. I placed my feet on top of them and stuck my head through the oval hole at eye level in the panel.

In front of me, in the completely reflective wall of the room, floated a dollar bill. I had to screw up my eyes, as the bill was a couple of metres away from me. I then saw clearly that the head of Lincoln, which belonged on it, had disappeared. In its place I saw my own head. The odd lighting in the room drained the colour from my face and replaced it with the dull green of the bill. Strange shadows distorted the structure of my skin and hair, so that the bill looked genuine. Slightly tattered too, as though it had been in circulation for years.

I walked around the panel. On the other side it was a mirror from floor to ceiling, on which had been painted a dollar bill several metres across. In the middle was a large hole. The wall opposite reflected the now faceless bill, with at its centre the empty oval in which I had just been framed.

Later I heard that A.O. had bought the installation and had it removed from the Museum. Those with too much money who still want more, ultimately have no other choice but to turn themselves into money.

Non-verbal. She was now standing right in front of him. The tips of their noses were touching. Her face was reflected in his. She saw her own nose on his skin in a strange, splayed shape. Her familiar freckles, which she knew from mirrors as a cluster of dark dwarf stars, could only be seen normal size on the bridge of his nose. On the nostrils of the Narcissist Guru™ they were distorted into spreading droplets of brown ecoline in water. Nothing of his own skin could be seen; everything was hidden by the reflective make-up.

She turned her head so that her right eye came so close to his left eye that their eyelashes tickled each other. While out of the corner of her eye she saw the freckles regain their normal proportions in the side of his nose and her nose was almost perfectly reflected in his, she opened her eyes wide. She was looking straight into her own iris, mirrored in the reflective contact lens. All that was visible of him was a fine strip of the white of his eye.

He closed his eyes for a moment and showed her the reflection of her iris on his eyelid. She put a hand on his neck and bent his head slightly downwards. Each of his hairs acted as a tiny, elongated mirror, and in the surface of his immaculately combed hair her face re-emerged, like a silver wave generated by the sea. He raised his head a little and she kissed him, but he recoiled.

She started. Right across his mouth was the imprint of her lips, where his own skin had become visible. She wiped her mouth with the back of her hand. The smear on her hand felt cold and greasy, and reflected her wide-open eyes.

He retreated further and left the room, taking with him her distorted and shrinking reflection with him on his back and legs.

'I reflect the world and the world reflects me,' said the Narcissist Guru™.

The self-conscious orgy. They stood admiring themselves in the mirrored walls in the sultry build-up to an auto-orgy. The cause of their boundless self-love was clear the moment I entered: these young men and women were classical beauties, as if the sculptures of Michelangelo had come to life. My entrance was not noticed.

I hesitated for a moment; wondered whether I should take notes or record conversations with my mobile. Some of the beautiful people had meanwhile started undressing. Items of clothing were flying about.

One girl, with a gossamer-thin build and the severe DNA of a fashion model in a tanga, with hair like the delicate cascade of a black marble fountain, raised her arms and surveyed her gyrating hips – or the place where they should have been – and the contour of her small breasts.

A young man, now also naked, pumped up his biceps and looked in the mirror from under his eyelids, frowning. Again and again he rearranged his limbs into new poses, and admired the result from head to toe.

Seventeen exceptionally beautiful people were admiring themselves, then, oblivious of each other.

I retreated, back to the room I had come from, and bumped into him there.

'They're waiting for me,' he said, 'so that they can admire themselves in me. Isn't that a social form of narcissism: seeing yourself in the other?'

He strode towards the door. I stared at my image on his back, while the narcissists gave cries of assent at the entry of their hero, the Narcissist Guru™. Before the mirrored door closed I saw a girl with her mouth wide open moving her head forwards and backwards, as if she were performing fellatio without a partner. She was observing herself intently in a mirror. Her groans were groans of admiration of what she saw, she was groaning with pleasure at this autobiographical porno.

The symmetrical creation. 'And I should now like to present to you our master: the Narcissist Guru™.'

The audience applauded the man in his reflective outfit, and all-reflecting skin, as a figure of liquid silver.

'The creation from which we all issue, has always given rise to questions. So much so indeed that the Darwinians felt compelled, on the basis of fossil evidence, to declare it invalid. As if a dinosaur and a hominid named Lucy justify that opinion!'

The television cameras and webcams gazed impassively at him.

'I have found what theology has looked for for so long. I

hereby declare that they have been proved right and that the Darwinians have been proved right. Yes, there is a creation. And yes, there is such a thing as evolution. But the two could never meet because the link was missing. Can there be such a thing as the proto-human Lucy in the family tree of Adam and Eve? And can dinosaurs roam an earth without humans?'

He paused for a moment, allowing the murmur to ripple through the room.

'I say to you: yes, it is possible by virtue of the missing link... the mirror!'

With arms outstretched the man indicated the mirrored walls on either side of the stage.

'Place a mirror in front of the opening lines of Genesis and you have the answer. We live in the reflected version of creation. In *our* eyes creation, paradise and Adam and Eve and the apple represent the beginning. In the original version, they are the end.'

In the vast ensuing silence a manuscript fluttered from his reflective coat tails, like a clown entering from the wings of a circus.

'In our reflected creation primitive man and the dinosaur have still yet to happen. They were not our precursors, but will come after us in a distant future. In a Third Testament that has been lost, or is yet to be written.

I say to you: creation may look like chaotic madness. A pointless spilling of blood in endless, virtually pointless sacrificial rituals. But only when every thing is mirrored is perfect symmetry created. One murder is a horrific act. But mirror the event and you have a perfect, symmetrical murder. Every action, every detail, every drop of blood, every sound and every sensation is duplicated and completely symmetrical.'

He held up the manuscript in front of him, sheet upon sheet of spindly writing and began reading it aloud.

'God had always called the light Day and the darkness Night. And God saw that it had been good and made the division between light and darkness undone. And there was no more light; and God spoke no more of the light. His Spirit moved upon the face of the waters. Darkness was upon the face of the deep and the earth was without form and void. And earth and heaven were finally ended by God.'

He stopped, raised his head, and cried forcefully; 'This is exactly where we place the mirror. And hence this is exactly where the mirrored creation, the part that we are now living through, begins, with the words *In the beginning God created the heaven and the earth.*'

Passage from an obituary. No art critic did more for the Narcissist Guru™ than Elijah Moody. In his obituary Moody writes, for example: 'There are two ways of giving light; by being the candle, or the mirror that reflects it. Layos Ladros was perhaps the perfect embodiment of the ideas of Descartes, who claimed that having knowledge is having representations in one's consciousness. Ladros goes a step further: through his mirroring manifestation he has himself become a representation.'

'He has also taken up a political position by arguing, in his essay *A Mirror for Marx, Engels and Lenin*, that we must not find reality by starting from reflections in the mind, and then reasoning our way laboriously back to reality. Something that the above trio considered dangerous. Ladros believed on the contrary that man should reflect what reality offered. By literally 'representing' one's surroundings one creates clarity. The citizen who reflects the violent behaviour of a KGB officer, learns more about crime than someone who shuts themselves off from it.'

'Ladros wept on his deathbed, because he had never got round to the mirrored version of *Mein Kampf*. He wanted to undo the horrors of the twentieth century by mirroring them.'

The organic mirage. Layos Ladros, the Narcissist Guru™, is still waiting for us in the desert outside the town where he became famous. Perhaps you will drive there one day. On any clear day, the immense figure of the Narcissist Guru™ is visible above the rolling landscape. Quivering in the heat of the desert, completely transparent, he stands with his hands piously folded looking down into the imaginary pool that showed Narcissus his fatal reflection. Somewhere beyond the sand dunes he floats in nitric acid in a transparent cylinder. The polished walls of his glass coffin act as magnifiers and enlarge his figure. The fierce sunshine and rising water vapours of the desert project his image high in the sky.

From miles away the pilgrim can enjoy the figure towering benignly above the desert.

The image of a man who reduced the whole of mankind to its essence: the mirage of a presumed existence.

***

Sketches of a Worldwide Christo and Jeanne-Claude

Hiding the Sahara from the Sun. I saw the sun fall. The thousands of students, professors, scientists, technicians, biologists, climatologists, electricians and others involved in the project were scattered across the desert. As far as the eye could see they were standing on trestle-shaped ladders and on the slopes of the sand dunes. They were awaiting the signal, an electrically amplified version of Richard Strauss's 'Also Sprach Zarathustra' for solo horn. Then, completely in synch, they switched on the thousands of electric winches suspended above them on posts scores of metres high. The winches pulled on thousands of polypropylene ropes, setting in motion the rolled-up fabric hanging between the posts. Because of its strange colour the fabric, although woven from polypropylene, looked like the authentic material used by nomads since time immemorial to erect their Bedouin tents beneath the merciless sun. It had the same seams, let the light through in the same way and had the same colour, which depending on the light could vary from grey-brown or dark blue to black. The woven fabric had been rolled up like a carpet, and attached to the tops of the iron tent poles, driven deep into the loose earth.

The distance between the poles was approximately fifty metres, whatever direction you looked in. As far as the horizon the desert was covered with these symmetrical rows of posts, like a forgotten frame for reinforced concrete, lost in time.

The tent poles followed the contours of the dunes. They always rose three or four metres or so from the sand. The fifty-metre rolls of fabric had been hung up on posts parallel to the horizon and were all unrolled at once and in the same way. Ropes were attached to the rolls of fabric at ten-metre intervals. The traction of the electric winches on the ropes caused the fabric to unroll.

Below, close to the sand, the fabric lengths joined at a height of only a few metres and were fixed together by Velcro edging.

In this way, in just a few minutes a new dark desert floor was created, from the sand dune where I was standing to the horizon. The fabric of this gigantic Bedouin tent was as undulating and steep as the dunes beneath it – like a perfect copy of the sand contours suspended a few metres above them.

This sudden rise in the desert, in the last few hours before sunset, created the illusion that the sun was in free fall. It was a short fall, but an unmistakable one.

From the hilltop, latitude 13° E – longitude 27° N, we

looked towards the horizon, at the last embers of the setting sun. The sand dunes of the Sahara had been covered by the gigantic creation. Their capricious contours had been completely obscured from view and straightened into an orderly Bedouin tent with the tips of the supporting tent poles at regular intervals. The artists stood beside me, feet apart, gazing at the fabric, over which the ridges were casting long shadows. They waved at the thousands of workers, who had emerged from under the fabric in order to climb the hill we were standing on.

In those last few minutes of twilight I was sure the sun had actually jumped down and so had skipped a fraction of our precious time.

From the production log. Materials required for the Sahara Tent: 80,000 km polypropylene rope, 3 million square miles of woven polypropylene fabric, 135,000 iron tent poles, 28,000 winches, 70 piledrivers, 4 million iron rings for securing the rope, 16 trailers and trucks, 30 helicopters for impassable terrain, 900,000 concrete anchor posts for the outside of the tent. The operations were preceded by 16 years of preliminary discussions with governments and local authorities, environmental groups and media, and 100,000 man hours were required for completion. Construction and dismantling takes 3 months up to the return of this area of the Sahara free of any trace.

Under a different sky. We spent the following days in the gigantic Bedouin tent. The media had descended on the edges of the area of three million square miles, extending between latitude 10°W – 30°E, and between longitude 10.5°N – 30°N. Convoys of landrovers with trailers and trucks containing mobile television studios and satellite dishes on their roofs, had left the motorway from Tripoli and were parked on the verge on the plateau from where there was a view of the work of art. It had been given the title 'Sahara Tent'. In the electronic announcement that had found its way across the world in the month preceding the installation, the artists described the purpose of the object.

'Humanity has wrapped things up since antiquity. Mummies are just one example of the naturalness of wrapping. The wrapped object is not exhibited in isolation in a museum, since museums precisely screen art off from the public space, thus severing the life-giving blood vessels between art and reality. The wrapped object should exist in and consist of real space itself, the world we live in. Each object is protected by the wrapping; in this case we are shielding the Sahara from the lasciviousness of the sun. For us, human spectators, wrapping is the only way of learning to see things with new eyes. The Sahara is as old as humankind, and no longer holds any mysteries for us. People consider such an arid region unusable, and a nuisance. By wrapping it, we are giving back the Sahara its mystery and will once again long for its mournful and eternal beauty. Wrapping is also a homage, a token of concern for the object.'

I stood next to the artists' trailer and stared at the undulating sea of tent cloth. The voice of an American television presenter wafted in my direction. He was standing with his back to the Sahara Tent and screwing up his eyes was looking into the lens of the camera on the shoulder of a cameraman, with the microphone, the fetish of his professional life, in his hand. Then he began: 'It has already been announced by NASA that this *Christo and Jeanne-Claude* – dubbed the Sahara Tent – is the second object after the Great Wall of China to be observable from space. Stay tuned. After this message from our sponsors, we'll be back with you with the first satellite images, which we have been able to secure exclusively for you.'

There was a commercial break. The presenter, a tanned forty-year-old with firm skin and sleeked hair that gleamed in the sun above an immaculate blue sports jacket and a dusty pair of jeans – invisible to the camera – abruptly lowered his mike. The crew bustled about. They started running to and fro, fiddling with the satellite dish and the presenter's hairdo, and amid all the activity no one noticed the wind getting up.

Above the voices I heard the grating sound that the sand made as it brushed the tyres of the trailer. My trouserlegs started flapping. I pulled my hat firmly on my head and began the descent to the Sahara Tent.

Twenty minutes later, at the bottom of the cliff at the foot of a steel staircase built for the public with an awning that gave protection from the sun, I reached the edge of the canvas. The wind did not reach here. The tent cloth hung at most two and a half metres above the sand. As soon as I stepped beneath it, I found myself under a different sky.

Here the time of day no longer mattered. The fierce light of the sun, almost directly above us, was filtered by the fabric. I took off my sunglasses and hat and felt a cooling breeze stroking my temples. The enormous polypropylene tent, with its dark shade, had succeeded, in these early hours of the day, in retaining something of the intense nocturnal cold of the desert.

By this time, eleven in the morning, the temperature would normally have risen as high as forty degrees. It must be twenty degrees cooler in here. The light varied, weakened here and there by the shadows of the sand ridges. A rainstorm seemed to be hanging over me, a dense artificial layer of cloud. Everywhere the fabric rose and fell, upwards from a few metres above the sand, and down from the vertical tent poles. To make it easier to view the work, the artists had had the poles numbered and attached direction signs. The route led further into the desert, deep into the tent. In front of me and behind me walked diplomats, military personnel and television people. Some did nothing but look up and around them, others stopped at each hill to say something into a microphone or to camera.

After an hour of wading through sand I reached a location set up for a break. We were received by a number of Tuareg, who had provided some water, a light meal and easy chairs and hundreds of one-person tents for a slightly longer rest. In this mysterious, silent world the Sahara Tent seemed to have reproduced itself and to be sheltering its young under its enormous wings.

In the evening large fires were lit by the Bedouin, Christo en Jeanne-Claude's guests-of-honour in their latest creation. The smoke escaped through specially made holes in the fabric high above us. They played camel-skin drums and accompanied their slow rhythms with deep, long-drawn-out guttural sounds. They looked up regularly, astonished nomads alarmed by the first echoes of their voices.

Tears in a sea of sand. I had been wandering for days beneath the Sahara Tent. There were several stopping-off points en route, arranged like the first, and scores of people wandered with across the terrain, drawn by the strange beauty. An inescapable beauty too, because I could not be the only one with feet covered in blisters and a sense of desolation. Here we were sheltered from time. The fabric tempered the fierce rays of the sun during the day, but during the hours of darkness seemed to amplify the moonlight, creating a strange twilight and blurring chronology.

On one of those days (from my notes I can deduce that it was afternoon) I was sitting on a camp chair on the edge of a stopping-off point deep beneath the tent. There were not many people left – I was one of the tenacious few, who did not know when to stop. The object had a limited life – like many of their twentieth-century works: the wrapped Reichstag in Berlin and the Pont Neuf in Paris, Surrounded Islands in Biscayne Bay, Valley Curtain in Colorado, Running Fence in California and others. In less than two weeks they would start dismantling the Sahara Tent, but I refused to think about it. Perhaps I wanted to drown my sun and moon-driven existence here in a sea of oblivion, and as I stared ahead, my mind a blank, I felt a tap on the head. I thought it was a fly and waved my hand above my head.

A drop fell on the back of my hand. I narrowed my eyes and

looked up. A few metres overhead was a fine mist of condensation droplets suspended from the underside of the tent fabric.

Historical footnote. *No research records have been found in which the sudden change of climate in the area beneath the Sahara Tent is described. The preceding and following notes that have been recovered are not confirmed by official sources. Climatologists accepted the theory that the very tiny amount of condensation traditionally found in the Sahara, under normal circumstances rises with the rapidly heating air, and is carried down to the equator. Christo and Jeanne-Claude's polypropylene fabric must have had an unexpected side effect: it retained literally virtually all condensation. In the two short weeks that the project lasted so much moisture was returned to the soil, that organisms that had been lying dormant for scores of millennia were able to seize their chance and flower.*

The tent of Eden. The two weeks had passed and there was still no sign of dismantling. The tent fabric hung impassively above me. For days I had been following the way back, using the signs fixed to the tent poles, resting at one stopping-off place after another, and still did not meet a soul. Beneath my feet the earth had opened up, making way for tiny shoots of desert flora. Arid, hard bushes with threatening thorns and no leaves. Buds had appeared on some runners, flowers gleaning with condensation waiting for the removal of the tent cloth, so that they could again profess their love for the sun. The few rocks in the area were covered in delicate mosses, which looked fluorescent green in the diffuse moonlight. Around me a shy savannah was hesitantly emerging, in which a few snakes and lizards were clumsily making the foliage rustle.

Heartened by the growth of this new covered Garden of Eden I walked through the gentle mist of condensation dripping down from the tent cloth towards the point where my journey had begun; a wandering Adam in search of his forgotten Eve.

Brave New Public Space. I was sitting on the folding stairs of my trailer staring at the tent landscape that stretched away from the foot of the plateau. It was pleasantly cool inside, but I could not abandon the work of art for long, and as I did every day, I had gone outside at first light. Above the polypropylene hung the sun, impassively, and as usual, with temperatures of 40°C and above, the air was shimmering. The red-hot aluminium of the trailer stairs burned right through my shoes and cotton shirt. But my face was brushed by a cool, moist current of air, so faint as to be scarcely perceptible. It seemed only a matter of time before this wind was actually able to cool me down, and the same went for this expansive anvil of the unrelenting equatorial blacksmith.

In the months since I had crawled out of the Sahara Tent made by the artistic couple, the humidity level under the fabric had steadily risen. The first vapour drops from those days had caused mosses and tiny plants to sprout. In the course of the seven weeks that followed, the process continued. In a short time a tropical microclimate had grown up, with rich vegetation, which received back all the moisture given off during the day via the tent cloth, and so was able to survive.

There was no longer any way through in the sticky, steamy heat. Deep marsh-like pools had been created between the sand dunes, swarming malarial mosquitoes, where you could disappear in quicksand at any step, and where the exceptionally high humidity took your breath away. Over the slopes of the dunes dense undergrowth had sprung up, where the original thorny desert bushes vied for space with rain forest vegetation, which you needed a machete to cut your way through. Various groups of researchers, scientists and art specialists went on such journeys, and both their eye-witness accounts and their official reports gave the same picture: in seven weeks the whole area of three million square miles had become saturated and fertile. They found that the sun could not maintain its impact on the soil at its old level. Under the fabric all plants had a strange, brown-purple colour, these were the colours remaining after the polypropylene had filtered out the sun light. A surreal garden, in faded Technicolor.

Since the first effects were noticeable within the two weeks that this Christo and Jeanne-Claude piece officially lasted the authorities of Algeria, Egypt, Lybia, Mali, Mauretania, Niger, Sudan and Chad had decided to postpone dismantling of the object. Christo and Jeanne-Claude had reluctantly agreed, because they did not want to ascribe any other role to their work than that of 'the public space as a work of art'. But the greenhouse effect that was unmistakably changing the planet, could use a counterweight, and if their art could coincidentally contribute, then so be it.

***

Territory Game

The land lay flat and desolate in the night, spurned by the cold starry sky, reflecting the pallor of the moon, and so it remained immutably until the first phase of sunrise. But as soon as the heavenly body revealed its first contours on the horizon and warmed the earth with its rays, the area gradually took on colour. Under the sun's loving touch, the white pall slowly lifted and was replaced all the way from the horizon by a clumsy palette of colours, consisting initially of nothing but stripes. Each ray of sun conjured a primary colour from the prism. Together they formed short rainbow-coloured lines that moved slowly across the white surface.

In fifteen minutes, the whole area was stripped of its nakedness and filled with millions of rainbows standing bolt upright. As the sun climbed higher they began to merge and produced rivulets of colour. These still pristine streams no longer ran in straight lines from the point where the sun had risen, but meandered ever more dramatically and here and there flowed into each other. At those points, seething pools of colour formed. The primary colours of the spectrum were extinguished in the birth of millions of intermediate shades. From yellow and blue came green. From red and blue came brown, from brown and white came the colour of sand, the colour of sand and green-orange produced still new combinations. The pools swirled like vortices till there were no more rivulets, and spread out till between them they covered the once deathly white land with a blanket of coloured patches. Each patch pulsated and undulated in the reviving warmth of the sun.

A road led towards a point on the horizon, somewhere below the position of the sun. The black tarmac stood out sharply against the soft, rippling pools of colour on either side of the road. A car approached over the road gleaming in the sun. The vehicle drove sedately down the middle of the road. The passengers, a woman at the wheel, and a little girl beside her, looked at the verges stretching in front of them. Ahead, the colourful flat landscape started to move. In the distance, the bio-polyester topsoil of this artificial terrain reacted to the vibration of the tyres and the sound waves and heat of the engine.

It was a powerful reaction. The flat ground first formed small sprouts that shot upwards before curling towards the sky like huge tentacles waving grandly to and fro and expanding. As the skin of each tentacle began to split and assume the pock-marked brown texture of tree bark, new branches sprouted from every trunk. Hundreds of branches forked and spread out in all directions like a discharge of globe lightning. Concurrently, flat and leaf-shaped excrescences grew every few centimetres. From the tip downwards, these leaves filled with a fresh light-green colour, intoxicated with the sunlight they were eagerly absorbing.

Every tree surging up from the flat land had its own bark structure and was adorned with different leaves. There were oaks, elms, beeches and birches. Some trees formed blossoms, or grew billions of needles. The ground between the trunks pushed up slightly to form a carpet of grass, initially the colour of the pools, but soon colouring fresh-green again from the tips of their blades.

As the car drove on, this dense and real-looking forest shot up in the time that it took the car to cover ten or fifteen metres – and disappeared behind the car with the same speed. A dissolving miniature world, whose colour had vanished even before it lost its form. Twenty metres behind the car the landscape had reverted to its original flatness and its colourful pools.

The woman suddenly pulled off the road, between two trunks, and parked on the grass. The trees in this spot instantly lost their foliage. While the leaves, which as soon as they started to fall exchanged their fresh green for atmospheric autumn red, fluttered around the car, the trees collapsed, till only the grass remained. All this happened in the few seconds the girl required to get out of the car. Now she danced among the leaves, which were changing from red to yellow ochre. Her mother turned off the ignition, then followed. They stood in the empty landscape, surrounded by a circle of grass twenty or so metres across.

The girl laughed so loudly at the last remaining leaves,

which seemed to be melting into the grass, that it triggered a new reaction in the landscape. Around them new shoots spiralled upwards, with dark green hairy stalks crowned by swelling buds. Thousands of them sprang up at a time, around them, close enough to be touched, but far enough away not to hurt them. In a few seconds the trunks grew to a height of approximately two and a half metres. Then all activity ceased. The sea of unopened sunflowers seemed frozen in a sudden, temperate ice age.

The girl watched wide-eyed and motionless.

'Mummy?' she asked

Around her the stalks trembled as if a breeze were blowing through them.

'We'll open them,' the woman said, 'Let's dance and sing.'

The child burst into cheerful song and leapt about, and while her mother took hold of her hands and they danced, the buds opened around them. First the buds nearest to them, in a circle around them, then the next ring, then the next a mass of unfolding sunflowers fanning out like paint thrown into a pond from a tin.

Then the mother lifted up the laughing and singing girl and threw her in an arc, so that she landed in the gently swelling sea of sunflowers. The child hung there for a while, screaming with pleasure till things quietened down and the flowers began shrinking for want of stimulus, and she finally dropped gently onto the grass as it drained of colour.

On the horizon, to the left of the point where the sun had risen, the airport buildings towered. A mounting roar signalled the takeoff of a large aircraft, and it clearly attracted the attention of the landscape. From all directions shoots of colour converged on the airport, the place from where the gigantic, top-heavy airliner was taking off. The shoots ranged from dark purple to black, gleaming like oil, with occasional bright yellow highlights. Like shafts of lightning they made for the space where the plane hovered in the air. There the landscape rose in convulsions of the earth, wild and chaotic. At first it rose a few metres at a time, then scores of metres, as if it were trying to touch the aircraft. The higher the plane climbed, the greater the gap the landscape strove to bridge.

Once it had climbed to a hundred metres the earth rose to that height in a trice, to just below the undercarriage. The upward surging mountain landscape turned grey and brown and black and red. Gigantic plateaus rose many metres in a fraction of a second. A huge mountain range swelled in the wake of the climbing aircraft, jagged peaks and sheer cliffs, shallow undulating gullies and deep ravines. Finally the plane veered left and crossed the limit of the bio-polyester landscape. At its extreme edge the landscape threw up a 3,000-metre mountain, which in a final act opened up a snow-covered volcanic crater.

But it was too late for flames; the thunderous engines and heat of the aircraft ebbed away, and the landscape subsided. As rapidly as it had risen, it had levelled itself out again and its colours had drained away into pools like painters's palettes: colours running together, without bounds, without territory, without name, without a fixed destination. The landscape bled dry as quickly as it had saturated itself with colour.

In the afternoon the sky clouded over. The landscape reacted by diluting its colours, since the light had now become too weak for complete coloration. Snow began to fall gently from the clouds. This seemed to make the landscape unsure of itself. The first flakes could scarcely touch the ground: the material of the soil tried to retreat, creating miniature craters. Then it began spewing back each flake, so that the landscape was soon splashing and seething like a lake in cloudburst. The flakes danced and in and out of them danced their partners, which were being forced upwards by the earth.

Now the terrain recovered. It had soon acclimatised to the cold. Here and there it threw up snowmen alongside a passing car with children in the back seat, and spewed snowballs at a few wayward youths crossing the bio-polyester terrain on mopeds.

In the evening, when the clouds had cleared, a Chevrolet pulled up at the side of the road. After sunset the landscape had lost its shape and colour and lay waiting for the moon. It reacted feebly to the car, forming a few abortive trees, but did not bother to make sunflowers.

The passengers got out. A young man and a young woman walked round the car. The boy sat on the bonnet, while the girl stood between his legs, and he began kissing her. She wrapped her arms round his lumberjack shirt and ran her fingers through his hair.

Around them the landscape came to life. In the ground something glowed red, like a fire smouldering underground. Lengths of wood shot out of the ground like hastily blooming tulips and flames licked around them. Bushes wound upwards, top-heavy with blossoms that sparkled purple in the car headlights. Insects took off from the ground, buzzing bio-polyester bees headed straight for the blossoms.

The girl took a step back when the boy took out a packet of cigarettes. As he put a cigarette between his lips and held a lighter to it, she said: 'Hey, on that notice it said no smoking or naked flames.'

'Who gives a FUCK?' the boy said.

He cocked his thumb to operate the lighter, but paused in mid-action to add a further comment.

'I wouldn't mind playing a territory game with my pocket knife here,' he laughed.

The land shuddered.

***

Beloved Stalker

The voice issuing from the telephone comes from far away in time. Yet the sound has scarcely changed in the decades that have passed since the words, "Mrs Four, I've rescued your womb from the hospital waste."

The old woman the voice is speaking to is standing at the table by the pool. The garden embraces her, and the wall embraces the garden, providing shelter from the Atlantic wind. The house nestles quietly among rose bushes, rhododendrons and the lawn; the white walls and awnings show respect for the sun, but the air conditioners by the windows on the terrace hum their protest at the climate.

The voice speaks slowly in her ear, lower than in the past, but still retaining melody and diction and a full stop at the end of each sentence – the voice of a man who still knows how to speak in proper periods.

"There was once a young opera singer for whose favours all the men in the world fought, but she found all of them too dull. They couldn't arouse her curiosity. Only one man succeeded in this. She met him at a chateau during a reception in the presence of the crown prince of Monaco, and she nearly died with longing to discover who he was and what he was like. She imagined, as only a true opera singer can, that one of her heroes from the librettos had come to life: Boris Godunov, or Peter Quint from The Turn of the Screw."

The old woman sits down. As she does so, the shadow of the years passes across her face. Only when she is seated do the creases and furrows and blotches in her face settle back into reasonably neutral terrain and she interrupts him. "Even after all these years you still always begin with 'there was once', just as you used to. But for some reason your stories refuse to turn into fairy tales."

"Mrs Four, I would so like to see your tattoo one more time. For the last time, while I still can."

The way he pronounces her name, softly, with a 'foo' sound, makes the old woman smile, as if she is seldom addressed in that way. But the smile is extremely short-lived.

"You're a tormentor. For fifty years you've let me think I was rid of you, and now, now that I'm too old to go on hating you, but too young to forgive... now you ring me."

"Have I insulted you for not calling for so long, Mrs Four?"

The woman moves her jowly jaws and a frown spreads above her eyebrows. The wrinkles form a completely new labyrinth with different angles and passageways, in which time can once more lose its way.

"Funny how often I've thought about what I would say if you showed up again, and now I've forgotten."

"I'm sorry," he says.

"Well then, tell me something, like you used to at the beginning, when you could still manage to be charming. You wanted to please me then."

"You were young. It was easy."

"Speak."

"Right. You were the youngest diva in the world and people flew from New York to Paris and from Johannesburg to Sidney to see you. You were the only person allowed to touch Picasso's Guerníca in front of the TV cameras, under the watchful eye of the museum's director, who looked up at you admiringly. No wonder, since you would not have been out of place as a sculpture in his galleries: tall and broad in the way that Picasso sculpted his women, and with a face framed by a cascade of black hair and a wide mouth that gave men the impression you were smiling at them and made women on the other hand doubt whether you were. When you sang, the traffic around La Scala ground to a halt."

Boredom crosses the old woman's face as she listens. "That's enough. Tell me, why did you say "while I still can"? Why are you alluding to my age as if I'm at death's door?"

"You've misunderstood me. It's not you, but I that am dying."

"At my time of life that's nothing special. I hear it so often. Have you seen my tattoo before?"

"On your twenty-ninth birthday. You were holding a press conference on the beach in Cannes and I was so happy to get close to you. And then I saw it."

"You mean 'her'."

"Yes."

"I can't have been wearing much at the time, for you to be able to see my tattoo."

"Yes."

"She's got too old for that now, like me."

"No, don't say that. I still think you're beautiful, Mrs Four. I sometimes see you coming out of your house. I don't think other people recognize you any more, but I do."

"You thought the same back then too, but you still pestered me day and night with phone calls."

"Yes. With flowers too, though. Oceans of flowers."

"Only at the beginning." She rubs her cheeks, and her skin rolls ahead of her fingers like a sea of leather."Who on earth are you? When are you finally going to tell me? While you still can, to use your words."

There is no answer from the telephone. Her eyes scan the ocean, but there is no sign of life there either. "You were a cruel person. Was that really necessary? Why were you so cruel, when you began so sweetly? You were a man at a masked ball who came to elope with me. You said I would soon be able to see your face. I was so young… you pierced my heart twice, once when you stole it with your words and then when you spurned it."

"I'm sorry."

"You said that already."

"Now it's your turn to be cruel."

"I beg your pardon?"

"Yes, I was cruel, Mrs Four. Now you can be cruel to me."

"How can I do that?" The old woman is passionate now. "It was your words. You said you would be in the audience and would undress me with your eyes. You said that you would aim an arrow of love at my husband from a balcony while I was flirting with another man on stage in The Turn of the Screw. That you would… my womb… Did you hate me or did you hate my fame or were you simply raving mad? It's possible you know, I worked with Fassbinder, and I sometimes had my doubts about him." The old woman pauses for a moment, out of breath.

"Are you really dying?" she asks after a while.

"Yes."

"Is that what your doctor says?"

"Yes. I'm already in hospital."

"So you couldn't see my tattoo anyway, even if I let you? Even if I invited you now?"

"You're inviting me now, now it's too late?"

"Yes, I'm inviting you."

"So you really can be cruel. You and I are made of the same stuff, Mrs Four, just as I told you when you were young."

The woman hears squeaks and other sounds she cannot place.

"I'm sorry about all those times I hurt you."

"I prefer to remember the beginning, when you were good to me," she says.

"They don't write about you anymore because there are too many new stars. I can force them to write about you again.'

"You've done that once already. The whole world wrote about me when you staged attacks on other opera stars and sent letters to the papers saying how you wanted to impress me and more of that kind of hysterical attention-seeking."

"I never focused attention on myself. No one knew who I was, but your fame grew by leaps and bounds."

She side-steps the insinuation. "My fame is behind me."

"I've always admired you, because you deserved to be admired. I stood in St Peter's Square when you appeared on the balcony with the pope – the people were beside themselves, I've never experienced anything like it since. People hit themselves on the head, others threw bottled water around to cool each other down, and scores of them fainted. You need admiration. Oh, why did you retire from public life?"

"As if you didn't know. Anyway, is that all people want: to admire celebrities? Fame isn't deserved, it comes and goes. It strikes some people with the arbitrariness of lightning or a tropical storm. What's admirable about that?"

She sighs deeply, pauses for breath and then says, "You'd do better to admire your doctor."

"Who will admire you when I'm no longer around, Glorianna Four?"

"Voilà. You've finally called me by my first name. Well I never."

She hears his heavy breathing. Yes, he's an old man now. He too.

"You're dodging my question. But it's all right. There was once a composer who wanted to marry a beautiful Italian girl called Julie Guicciardi, but he couldn't."

"You're still showing off your knowledge. But what do you mean by that? Couldn't you show your true face, as you said, and is that why you became so cruel? Say who you are at last. Are you afraid? Do you have royal blood?"

The woman stares out over the ocean with the telephone to her ear, oblivious of time. She brushes her dress off nonchalantly, as if wanting to appear unmoved in case he is observing her from a great distance. The waves roll across great distances, and the moonlight is replicated in their foaming tops.

She is startled by a woman's voice, and has no idea how much time has passed.

"¿Hola? ¿Hola?" ("*Hello? Hello?*")

"Yes...?"

"Lo siento. Usted... El señor Lloria acaba de morir." ("*I'm sorry... You... Mr Lloria has just died.*")

"What's that... died? Señor... Lloria?"

"No ha sido inesperado, señora. No sufrió. Sucedió como había dicho el médico. ¿Puede mantenerse un momento en línea? Tengo que ir a por el buscar al médico." ("*It's not unexpected. He wasn't in pain. Things went as the doctor said they would. Would you hold the line for a moment? I have to fetch the doctor.*")

She hears receding footsteps down the telephone. The old woman presses the telephone hard against her ear, her eyes wide open as if they want to suck up information through black holes.

White strips mark the endless waves in the deep distance. The sky above the Atlantic Ocean is streaked with red above the horizon. When nothing happens for a while, she hangs up. It looks like a decision, but it is no more than a gesture.

***

Burning Neil Armstrong

We're so happy we can hardly count.
Roger Waters, *Have a cigar*

The pornocracy. Whores have sold our final resting place, the night. I am one of them. The hours of the moon and the stars are our last resort, where asylum is granted to refugees from the world of light. There we can rest, tired of hard labor, and enjoy the silence without having to deliver something in return. The darkness, that invigorating cool silence, is our priceless savior.

But we can do as we please, even if it goes against ourselves. Only one victim is indeed innocent, and I miss her already. Her sad, tired glow, that calmed many a tortured soul. Long ago she was already looking down on this emerging pornocracy, this reign of whores, and gave us absolution each and every night. I will miss her and her pale calm.

What has become of us? Once, a man wrote *Moon River* because he was set on fire by what he saw: the silver liquid dripping down from the moon, covering the shoulders of an introvert earth with a comforting robe. The song put us at ease. Now the heirs own the copyrights to that same *Moon River*, their business representatives wringing their hands at the prospect of a hundred years of royalties.

The world sings the same song but has itself changed beyond recognition. Once the world was like Elvis Presley, shivering while singing *Blue Moon:* —For she's my true love...

Once the world was like Louis Couperus, who shivered orgastically while he wrote what he saw:

—At night the moon pours a bath of cool and dew from its silver bowl...

But that was a long time ago. He didn't have to live through what we have to experience when we pay the admission tickets to some Lunar Park, where a polyester moon hangs from cables in a hall and a woman's voice imitates Frank Sinatra, her diction seemingly coming from nowhere:

–Móón river, wider than a mile...

Is there anything left that we don't do for money?

On the drip of figures. Today no one would go to battle the way people did in the twentieth century. The unwilling masses are now drafted with money to buy themselves food and games. Tanks, concentration camps and atomic bombs have lost; money is the winner. The greatest and strongest army has never achieved what the combined currencies yen, dollar, euro and renminbi achieve. The very same values that were once trampled by soldiers' boots are now expressed in amounts and currencies. The descendants of gypsies who were gassed by hate, are now expenses on the European governments' budgets. The wars themselves have been replaced by legal actions about money — on bank accounts and in art collections. Once robbed from their dead owners in an orgy of hate; now kept from their rightful owners by pure avarice. The courtrooms are the new battlefields of our time, where the fight over financial gain is a bitter one.

Once upon a time countries rolled across each other's territories, driven by a hunger for power. Now they buy each other's inventory without a single drop of blood being spilled.

God has witnessed the creation of money with sorrow and is putting off his intervention until the moment when the German government reissues *Mein Kampf* legally once again, in the hope the state's finances will benefit like never before. Osama Bin Laden chose the straight, glass towers of the wonderland where Alice spends her eternal adolescence — the rain that poured down was made up of figures more than tears. 2,700 dead, 100,000 tons of steel, 350,000 tons of glass, 600 billion dollars of damage to the worldwide economy.

We are lying on the drip of figures. For a long time now wars have been fought without weapons. Against South Africa, Iraq, North Korea, Cuba and the USSR economic sanctions took the place of conventional weapons. For new generations war is a borrowed memory. The wrongheaded and the rioters are cut off from the money-dripping breasts of the capital beast, or are instead cuddled to death by them. Of the moon, once a call for tragedy, romance and passion for poets and lovers, pieces of surface have been for sale since the nineties.

Feeling, expressed in units. Vincent saw the sun and wanted to capture her on the canvas. The value of painting lay before him in an ecstasy that became visible in the form of sweat drops on his forehead, in October 1888. Today the value of Van Gogh sunlight, converted to the total value of his works divided by the total acreage of the sunlight he painted, is: 1.2 million euros per square centimeter of canvas. To be sure, an amount that puts most people into ecstasy.

John Lennon wrote:

—I read the news today, oh boy.

His lyrics of *A Day in the Life* had a simple value when he created them: a rush of happiness flowed through his body, spreading to his wife, whom he came very close to that night, and to Paul, George and Ringo, who shared his heavenly lyricism. After that, the rest of the world followed. Today, the value of this line, converted to the Lennon/McCartney stock exchange IPO, would be roughly 3.78 million euros.

Since 2005 the value of the Lennon/McCartney stock exchange IPO has been seventeenfolded, thanks to merchandising. For the owners of a warehouse holding, *A Day in the Life* has double value. First they sell the music across the counter for a serious profit. Secondly the music, as it floats through elevators and floors full of riches, influences the warehouse visitors. The majority is brought into a positive mood by the music. To be more precise: they spend more and more money on products they need less and less.

In George Harrison's obituary the newspaper informs us about the amount of British pounds he leaves behind. That's all folks. Feeling, expressed in units.

Paranoia paloma blanca. When among people, you never say you think *Paloma Blanca* is a good song. Time's statistics say that those who fancy *Paloma Blanca* are millionaires considerably less often than aficionados of *Yesterday*, or *Strangers in the Night*, or *My Way*, with Sinatra's version scoring slightly lower than Presley's. Presley performs better on the list because the nouveau riche appreciate him more. *Paloma Blanca* is among the average, while fanciers of *Blueberry Hill* and *At Your Service* have extremely small prospects of becoming millionaires: only 0.004%. Readers of *The Osterman Weekend* by Robert Ludlum and *The Lily Theater* by Lulu Wang are at 0.02%, while people who own *Lolita* by Vladimir Nabokov, *Un saison en enfer* by Rimbaud and *The Strange Case of Dr. Jekyll and Mr. Hyde* by Robert Louis Stevenson are at the absolute top. Owners of *The Divine Madness* by H.R. Vlek or *Of the abyss and the sky man* by Lucebert are relatively low on the list.

There is no logic to be found in any of this. It is obvious, however, that no one possesses the capacity to be one's self any longer. Everyone is now their own capital.

Vogue economics. Outward beauty as a source of happiness has been outpaced by money. Since then fashion by Armani, Versace, DKNY, YSL and Prada has never been shown in front of the rich, but *by* the rich. On today's catwalk the wealthy billionaires walk. A tradition that still remains is for them to be beautiful, but it is no longer the only requirement. When the monitors above the catwalk project names like Kennedy, Branson, McCartney, Connery, Cruise, Reagan, Delon, waves of pleasure go through the audience. The thought of such wealth, shaped as endless estates and bank accounts across continents, relaxes the desperate. On the horizon the light of riches glows. You can never become beautiful like them, but you can be that rich.

Audience in the night. The architects, accountants, and lawyers of the Walt Disney Corporation have come up with the following. Instead of ten hours a day, every amusement park must henceforth be open twenty-four hours a day. During every hour when a park is closed, there is no return from the capital invested in roller coasters, haunted houses, and fairy tale castles. Of course this also meant that an audience had to be found for the hours of the night. In business terms: the corporation needed to create demand for the new, nocturnal product.

Wide awake for the super economy. For quite some time, three quarters of the adult population of the world has been plagued by insomnia. The step towards total absence of sleep is a small one. Super vitamins keep people on their feet for six days, twenty-four hours in a row. You can work nonstop. On and around the seventh day you sleep for thirty-two hours. No lack of sleep, no time off, maximum productivity. Because the world market is completely open, no country can stay behind.

Work councils and unions weaken as the economic climate improves. The past decades have shown endless growth, until every form of labor protection was drowned in the tide of wage increases. Luxury has anesthetized the masses, who have been apathetically staring at the hypnotizing shadows on their television screens, while the remains of consciousness resist the approaching end. The economic revolution rages without consent.

Powerless Africa and sulking Islamic countries have been ransomed with tidal waves of money. Protest movements have been compensated.

The unloving darkroom. For lack of a night, sleeping will have to be done in darkened rooms. During the past year, governments have built several millions of 'darkrooms': buildings full of rooms that are void of light and sound, and entirely focused on sleep. Sleeping at home will become infeasible for most people, because once the economy is operational on a round the clock basis (two nights from now!), no place on earth will really ever be quiet again. As an example: transportation will go on day and night, and of course no real train or truck can pass in complete silence. The dogs try to sleep as the caravan roars past. In that ear-deafening noise, relationships will become a thing of the past very soon, because people who work all the time will have no more time to court one another. And if they ever have the opportunity, and they're together, they will be too tired to make love anyway. From now on, love's arrows will turn away in full flight and be drawn into the black holes of the super economy: the darkrooms. Thanks to the super profits it has become financially viable to banish procreation to laboratories anyway.

Super food. For decades they've been cultivating food that never stops growing, even without the night to fold up its leaves. The new super plants can be harvested twice as many times. Among the breeds ready are Siberian rice, Taiwanese beans, Middle American grain and the Dutch nightingale potatoe.

Mankind has given away its position at the top of the food chain to money.

Economic orgasm. Now that the inventiveness of entrepreneurs has almost finished off the night, it is time to say goodbye to the moon. I'm joining Cornelia, Chuck, Jojo, and William, and we travel to a place where we can see the lady in her old appearance for the last time. We fly a Boeing, like a white bird through the second-to-last night, high up in the fluorescent night. I hum *Paloma Blanca* in this rushing Boeing cabin. No one hears it; they are all listening to the sounds of the stock exchange in their earphones. A man, his hands on his earphones, ejaculates, or so his orgastically jerking facial muscles say. It is most likely he is just being informed about a formidable raise of his stocks.

An inflating rate in an air pocket!

Perhaps later the man will find out the real story behind flying. It is not like someone is serving us, passengers, with a plane and a schedule flight and cabin personnel. It is the other way around. Someone is making money. The money streams towards him, actually, and to keep it that way his planes must continue to fly, around the globe without interruptions, and for that purpose people must get on board in exchange for payment.

There is no economy in the sea; there is no economy amongst elephants. Amoebae have no economy. We people, we no longer live for ourselves; we are but fodder for the economy. The economy has taken the place we have occupied for tens of thousands of years: at the top of the food chain.

If only the economy was suffering from bulimia. At least then we'd be thrown up.

The Bedouin fire. We have the right to one more natural day and we arrive on the equator, where camels lull us through a world of sand. Waves of copper-colored grains tower above us, or stretch around us in the deep, like windswept curtains on a caliph's court. Dark red robes envelop the camel drivers, who show only their ears and eyes to us: Cornelia, Chuck, Jojo, William and me. With those eyes the drivers see how I lived for money and bought friendships. How I had people chased out of their hovels by thugs and lawyers, to build expensive apartments and corporate headquarters in their place. We are all guilty and helped build the super economy.

Chuck gets his harmonica and we sing under his leadership.

—All things must pass, all things must pass away.

The bedecked men stoke a grand fire in the falling night and roast the only camel that wasn't carrying any passengers today. Flames rise from their own ashes and appear to be licking the darkened sky. Sparks drift upwards by the hundreds and mingle with their pale nephews and nieces, the stars. The sparks are young and fiery, later they will be like the stars: immortal, but without hope.

The moon. She climbs only when the rule of the night is complete; it is her last darkness.

The naked moon. She rises, like Louis Couperus' silver bowl, ignorant of her irreversible fate. Since time immemorial she's had this shape, the Sea of Tranquility has been on this spot. We have been thinking we see a face. We have been wanting to touch her astonishing clarity. The full moon changes the world beyond recognition. The copper yellow of the sand vanishes and is replaced by a sandblasted steel. Hard steel mountains surround us. Camels turn from yellow brown to dark blue, and the dark red robes of the Bedouins turn gray. My hands fluoresce, my nails radiate a bluish light that draws stripes in the night when I move them.

I stare at the moon. I think I recognize the Sea of Tranquility of photographs. That's the difference, I guess: the sun may also have places that deserve names. Mountains, valleys and oceans of fire. But you can't look at them with the naked eye. The sun hides itself behind the wall of light. The moon shows itself to us in all her nakedness. And she watches over us in the hours of the devil.

The firing squad. The flames want to go up, towards the moon. Tomorrow, they may. Tomorrow they will travel there. Tomorrow the NASA technicians will set the moon on fire, an interplanetary firing squad. Fossil fuels from the inside of the moon, nuclear fusion, combinations of both, it doesn't matter. They are so damned handy. They can do anything. From then on the moon will burn like a second sun and light the earth at night. The economy of the world will continue and the share prices can go up further. The parks of the Walt Disney Corporation will receive twice as many visitors. Warehouses and supermarkets will create turnover during the nights too. Road taxes can be doubled. People will have to eat and drink more because they'll almost stop sleeping. We will swallow more super vitamins.

Ernest Hemingway's debut will be republished with the new title *The Sun Always Rises* — because the stock exchange listed publisher smells a market for it.

The sun will always rise and set. But tomorrow the moon dies at the stake. The fine moon sand will melt in the intense heat and along with the disappearance of his footsteps our memory of Neil Armstrong will fade. We will forget that Neil never walked the moon because there was money to be made for someone. He walked the moon because his dream of a better world drove him and others into space. Now we wander around in this self-made nightmare. Blinded by the sea of fire we search for the lost footsteps of Neil Armstrong, which will show us the way home.

***

Request from the author

Thank you for reading this short story collection. I hope you enjoyed it and will be willing to write a review on Amazon. Making that extra effort is greatly appreciated by other readers... and of course by me. Thank you!

You can also follow me on Twitter or Facebook, or sign up for the free e-mail newsletter. I'll make sure you'll stay tuned.

Twitter @MHVesseur
Facebook www.facebook.com/MHVesseur
Subscribe to M.H. Vesseur's mailing list on www.mhvesseur.com

Have a good evening/night/day! I hope we stay in touch!

M.H. Vesseur

About the author

M.H. Vesseur has written many short stories for literary magazines in The Netherlands, Belgium, Canada and the U.S.A. He was awarded for the best debut with his first story. In his new series about bizz jockey and radio detective Carl Pappas he has now written and published the five short crime novels "CEO Groupie", "Die Rich", "Tax Me If You Can", "Acid Asset", "Nosedive" and "Power Play". Next he wrote the first book in the new series The Hitomi Files called "North", starring one of the main characters from the Radio Detective series. He also published the novel "Lemniscate". M.H. Vesseur is also an awarded advertising copywriter. Born in Hilversum, he now lives in Amsterdam, The Netherlands.

Visit:

www.mhvesseur.com

www.facebook.com/MHVesseur

Follow M.H. Vesseur on Twitter: https://twitter.com/MHVesseur

For news and more: subscribe to M.H. Vesseur's mailing list. Go to www.mhvesseur.com.

About the translator

Paul Vincent is a full-time translator who has published a wide variety of translated poetry, non-fiction and fiction, including works by Achterberg, Bernlef, Boon, Claus, Couperus, Elsschot, Jellema, Martinus Arion, Mulish, De Moor and Van den Brink. In 2010, he was awarded the Vondel Translation Prize for his translation of Lous Paul Boon's My Little War (Dalkey Archive Press, 2010).

About the short stories

In Snuff Park was first published in The Netherland in Nymph and in the USA by Mobius Magazine. It was also published as an Amazon Kindle ebook. **Babyface Junkie** was first published in The Netherlands in Nymph and in Canada by Descant Magazine. It was also published as an Amazon Kindle ebook. **Narcissist Guru** was first published in The Netherlands in Lava. It was also published as an Amazon Kindle ebook. **Sketches of a Worldwide Christo and Jeanne-Claude** was first published in Belgium in De Brakke Hond. It was also published as an Amazon Kindle ebook. **Territory Game** was first published in Canada by Descant Magazine. It was also published as an Amazon Kindle ebook. **Burning Neil Armstrong** was first published in The Netherlands in Nymph.

For original publication artwork visit:

www.mhvesseur.com

Available in The Hitomi Files by M.H. Vesseur
Ebooks and paperback, on Amazon, Apple iBooks and Kobo

NORTH

Man should fear only one enemy

The only enemy who has the capacity to remove all of mankind from the earth, is the virus. Imagine the worst of them all, a true 21st century killer. It lies dormant in the remote laboratory of a pharmaceutical giant whose hopes of making billions off a vaccine somewhere in the future throw a dark shadow ahead. Then Hitomi Sakamoto, the hard boiled radio producer who's on a rough vacation in the wild nature of the north, stumbles upon this dark secret. She is drawn into a final battle between ruthless scientists, a greedy corporation, desperate but dangerous environmental activists, a cold-hearted assassin and... a manmade virus that longs to escape.

Hitomi Sakamoto first appeared in the Radio Detective novels by M.H. Vesseur. Immediately popular for her iron work ethics and razorsharp tongue, Hitomi outgrew her boss (radio detective Carl Pappas) and now steps out of his shadow, into her very own adventure.

Available in the radio detective series by M.H. Vesseur

Ebook and paperback in the Amazon Store

CEO GROUPIE - A radio detective novel

One night three live guests join Carl Pappas on his radio show The Boardroom: two CEOs and a woman who calls herself: "the CEO Groupie". When the mysterious woman reveals the existence of a secret call girl organization for CEOs and subsequently disappears a couple of days later, the bizz jockey engages on a search. What happened to the CEO Groupie and what are the other two guests up to? Together with his radio team — his producer Hitomi Sakamoto and his sound engineer Don Wozniak — Carl Pappas sets out to deal with this.

Available in the radio detective series by M.H. Vesseur
Ebook and paperback in the Amazon Store

DIE RICH - A radio detective novel

Carl Pappas, the bizz jockey, goes on the air again. His radio show "The Boardroom" is both loved and feared by the global business community. He has a sharp eye for business news and the big mouth of a talk radio host. This time around he has some very wealthy guests joining him on his show: two billionaire entrepeneurs and their future successors, who also happen to be their sons. Of course it doesn't take the bizz jockey a very long time to upset some of his guests and his audience — and that same night the bizz jockey finds himself heading into dangerous waters, in the hands of some very angry rich people. His team — producer Hitomi Sakamoto and sound engineer Don Wozniak — is forced to go out and rescue their reckless boss. And then there are the rich kids they have to deal with...

Available in the radio detective series by M.H. Vesseur

Ebook and paperback in the Amazon Store

TAX ME IF YOU CAN - A radio detective novel

Carl Pappas, the bizz jockey, is cooking up a real shocker: during a live broadcast of his popular business talk radio show "The Boardroom" he plans to reveal secrets about tax dodging practices around the globe. In the middle of the preparations he and his producer Hitomi Sakamoto face unexpected trouble. Who is trying to shut the Bizz Jockey up in this quiet country under the tropical sun? Is it the local military junta? Is it the business community? Or is the sun finally getting to Carl Pappas' head?

Available in the radio detective series by M.H. Vesseur

Ebook and paperback in the Amazon Store

ACID ASSET - A radio detective novel

Carl Pappas, the bizz jockey, is feeling good about the prospects of environment-friendly plastics he's discussing on his radio show "The Boardroom". But as he soon finds out there's something not right with the company behind it. Can the bizz jockey protect a lonely scientist against the schemes of a large corporation that smells money? Or will he be unable to stop a revolutionary asset from becoming really acidic? Buckle up for a race against arsonists, corporate crime, dogs, bullets and a dangerous industrial zone in the middle of a blizzard, softened only by some real team spirit.

Available in the radio detective series by M.H. Vesseur

Ebook and paperback in the Amazon Store

NOSEDIVE - A radio detective novel

When a large corporation is struck by a cripling strike among its workers and an apparent terrorist attack on its factory, bizz jockey Carl Pappas steps forward to offer his public support.

But as he soon finds out, there's more to the picture than meets the eye. Why is the owner hiding in her large mansion? What happened in her youth that is threatening her after all these years? It's a job for the radio detective — and this time around his boss gives an unexpected hand.

Available in the radio detective series by M.H. Vesseur

Ebook and paperback in the Amazon Store

POWER PLAY - A radio detective novel

The death of an environmental activist brings bizz jockey and unofficial "radio detective" Carl Pappas to the quiet island of Islasol. Everything seems to be OK with the local National Park and the wind turbine park in the heart of it.

But Carl and his team soon find out you can't take anything on face value. Below the surface of an environment friendly enterprise lies a darker secret. It's time for the radio detective to unravel the local secrets of wind energy, assisted by his producer Hitomi and a new, unlikely ally.

Available in the radio detective series by M.H. Vesseur

Ebook and paperback in the Amazon Store

BLOOD BORDER - A radio detective novel

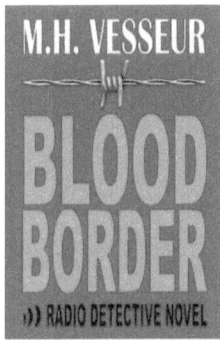

The inhumanity of human trafficking is forcing the radio detective to make a stand. So in the midst of politics and public outrage, Carl Pappas and his team infiltrate the trafficking cartel of a man known as The Clown. But there is nothing funny about it, for the radio detective soon finds himself in the lion's den, a place crowded with former narcotics traffickers and their violent ways. Will they be able to do something about the screaming injustice of immigration or will they become prey themselves?

<<<<>>>>

www.ingramcontent.com/pod-product-compliance
Lightning Source LLC
Chambersburg PA
CBHW031856170626
46807CB00004B/1751